CHINESE
PAPER CUTTING

CHINESE PAPER CUTTING

Diane Feng

Kangaroo Press

CONTENTS

Originally published in Australia in 1996 by Kangaroo Press
An imprint of Simon & Schuster (Australia) Pty Limited
20 Barcoo Street, East Roseville NSW 2069

This edition licenced in Great Britain 2002 by
Search Press Limited
Wellwood, North Farm Road
Tunbridge Wells, Kent, TN2 3DR

Printed through Colorcraft Ltd., Hong Kong

ISBN 0 86417 761 5

INTRODUCTION

Welcome to my paper cutting collection. Paper cutting is a traditional Chinese folk art, part of China's rich cultural heritage.

Even as China moves rapidly towards modernisation, there is still deep interest in the past. The art of paper cutting provides a window for Westerners to appreciate this past and also to find a fun and rewarding leisure-time pursuit.

The simple elegance that experienced practitioners of the craft achieve can surprise and motivate the novice. The themes can be conventional, such as people, animals or objects, or they can be abstract geometric forms. The size can vary from a tiny decoration for a cake to a large ceiling piece.

Paper cutting can be contrasted with Chinese painting—it shares the style of powerful simplicity but often has more vitality and is more accessible to the population as a whole.

The past

It was in China that paper was first invented and it is no surprise that the Chinese people have always enjoyed using it in varied ways. The art of paper cutting was an affordable but enjoyable craft that spread throughout China to almost every province.

When paper was invented during the Han dynasty, embroidery was a popular art and it is thought that paper cutting was first developed for use in creating embroidery patterns.

By the T'ang dynasty, it was a highly popular art form among both the nobility and the peasants. At the Spring festivals in T'ang dynasty China, courtiers from the Royal Court would appear carrying flags decorated with silver and gold paper cut-outs in the form of letters or flowers.

Unlike some other elements of Chinese art, paper cutting was open to women. In fact, it was considered an accomplishment for a young woman to be skilled in paper cutting—it could earn her the respect of her husband and his family.

Special paper cutting patterns might be passed down from generation to generation, and some families supplemented their incomes by selling cut-outs at markets or on special occasions.

Some cut-outs could take on mystical significance. The Chinese characters for luck, long life and happiness were popular cut-outs for bringing fortune to the family. In the Yuan dynasty, some believed that a cut-out of a female figure holding a broom would deter floods since she could sweep away the water.

The present and this collection

Paper cutting is being rediscovered and those who have kept the art alive are in demand. The patterns in this book have been designed by experienced practitioners of the craft to introduce you painlessly to paper cutting so that you can practise and learn it.

Traditionally, when Chinese people learn paper cutting, they start by cutting pre-printed patterns. As their skills increase, those who pursue the craft no longer rely on pre-printed patterns, but design in their heads as they cut. Using this book you can start the process. The cut-outs that you make from this collection can be used in many different ways—you can put them on your favourite books or paste them on windows or lampshades, for example. Glued down and protected with several coats of varnish, a set of cut-outs would make excellent decorations for coasters or table mats. You can create your own cards or use cut-outs as something different when you wrap a gift, either gluing them to plain paper or using them as stencils with craft spray paint.

Other variations include cutting the patterns from multi-coloured paper, as I have done with the Opera House cut-out on page 28, and using different colours for different parts of the design—the little pandas look good cut from black paper with the bamboo leaves cut from green paper, or the ball cut from orange paper.

Cut-outs can be framed and displayed on a desk or wall. How about tracing them onto fabrics or pillowcases and using them as embossing patterns for embroidery? As well as these many uses, I'm sure you will be able to devise your own interesting ones.

Diane

HOW TO USE THIS BOOK

This book has been designed to be used in two different ways.

1. The patterns printed in black should be photocopied before you use them so that the patterns on the other side of the page remain intact. Enlarge or reduce them as you wish.

2. The eight pages of patterns printed in colour can be taken from the book and cut out direct. Of course, if you wish to keep the book intact, these designs can also be photocopied.

Each design can be cut out as an individual piece, or produced as multiple copies (see page 17).

EQUIPMENT

1. A cutting board. You can use a sheet of heavy glass or a ceramic tile, a plate or even a small fruit-cutting board.
2. A cutting instrument, such as a one-sided razor or an artist's scalpel. These can be obtained at art supply shops, stationery stores or newsagents. The blade must be replaced regularly, or sharpened with a fine file, before it becomes blunt enough to risk tearing the paper. Traditionally, Chinese paper cutters used a special cutter which resembles an old-fashioned nibbed pen.

Sharp scissors can be used but they do not allow the same degree of control.
3. Access to a photocopier which makes clear precise copies.
4. A supply of good quality fine strong paper, in a range of colours, which can be cut without tearing or fraying. A range of suitable papers cam be found in art supply shops. Gift wrap can also be used.
5. A steady hand!

TECHNIQUES

Read this section in conjunction with the colour photographs on pages 17–18 and 27–28.

1. Place the cutting board in a stable non-slip position on a desk or table.
2. Take one of the pre-printed coloured pages from the book, or a photocopy of one of the designs.
3. Lay the design directly on the board, or staple it to 3–5 sheets of paper to make multiple copies.

4. Holding the cutter vertically and making small short cuts, cut out and remove all the white areas to leave only the pattern.
5. Sharp scissors can be used to trim the outer edge of the pattern, or you can finish off with the scalpel.
6. Use the finished paper cut-outs in the ways suggested on page 5, or place them in an album of your work.

PATTERNS FOR PHOTOCOPYING

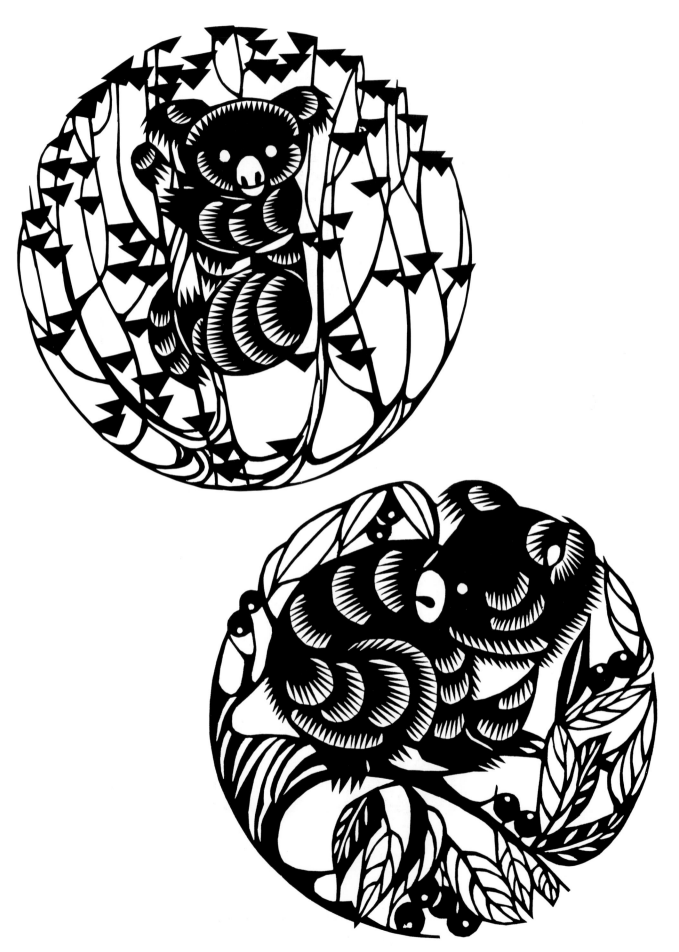

TECHNIQUES

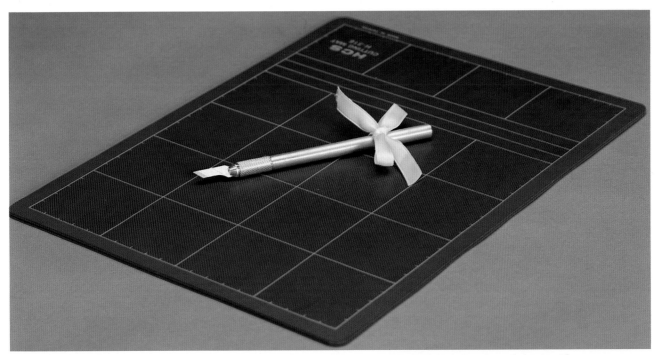

1. Cutting board and artist's scalpel. A one-sided razor blade can also be used, but avoid the kind of knife with snap-off blades

2. Stapling the pattern to several sheets of paper

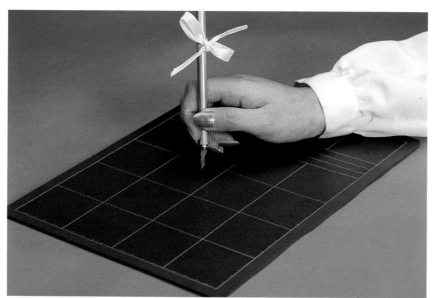

3. *The correct way to hold the cutter—always keep it vertical*

4. *Always make small short cuts. Push the cutter downwards vertically, making sure it cuts right through the paper stack. Pull the cutter upwards and towards you on the return to complete the cut. Do the small parts first. Cut out all the white parts to leave only the pre-printed pattern. The outer edge of the pattern can be cut with the scalpel or with a pair of sharp scissors*

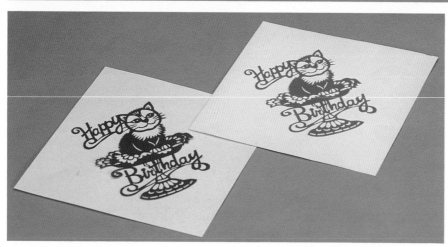

5. *The completed paper cuts laid on sheets of coloured paper*

PATTERNS FOR CUTTING

USING
PAPER CUTS

6. Framed paper cut of the Sydney Opera House (see page 38)

7. Budgerigar cut-outs used to decorate a table lamp (see page 7)

8. Paper cuts used on gift wrapping (see page 41)

9. Gift card. This design appears on page 39

10. Interesting effects can be obtained by cutting the designs in patterned paper. This design appears on page 38

PATTERNS FOR PHOTOCOPYING

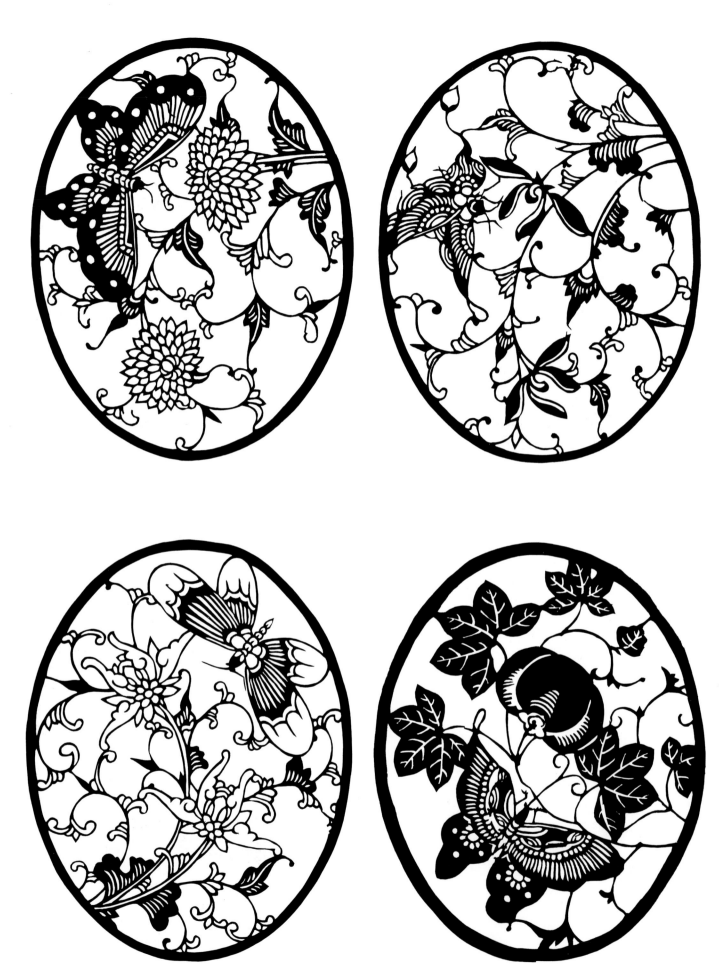